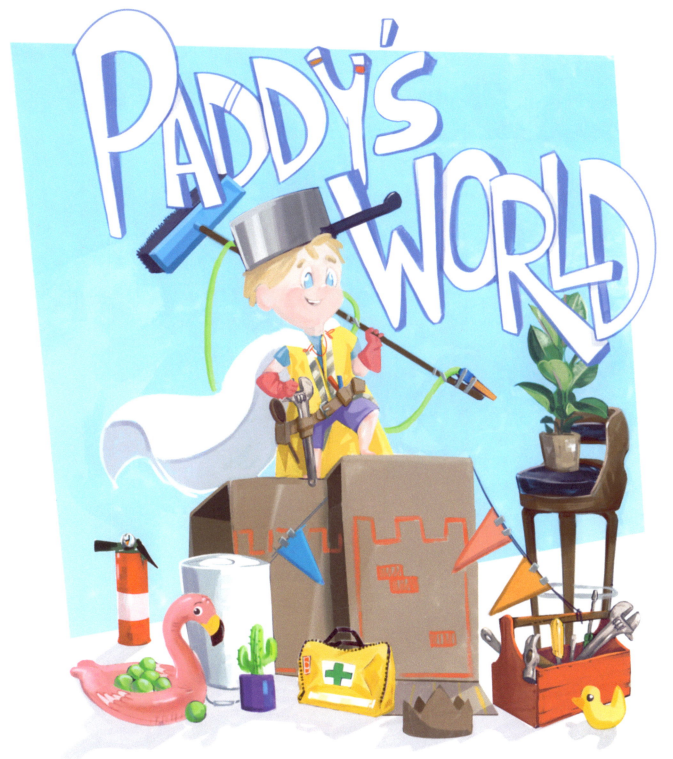

Paddy is an ordinary boy, living an ordinary life, on an ordinary street, in an ordinary house.

But he has a very extra ordinary imagination.

Monday

Today is no ordinary day.
Today is an extraordinary day.
Today Paddy is a doctor.

Wearing his stethoscope and scrubs, Paddy checks Mum's heartbeat ten times in a row, he rides the ambulance to the hospital and performs life saving surgery on his toy bear using an entire box of bandaids.

Tuesday

Today is no ordinary day.
Today is an extraordinary day.
Today Paddy is a penguin.

Paddy the penguin races his motorbike around the track, going over jumps, drifting through corners and narrowly missing spectators, leaving a trail of mess behind him.

Wednesday

Today is no ordinary day.
Today is an extraordinary day.
Today Paddy is a chef.

Preparing his favourite meal, Paddy helps in the kitchen measuring, pouring and mixing the ingredients, waiting for it to cook and serving it on plates. Then refuses to eat a single bite.

Thursday

Today is no ordinary day.
Today is an extraordinary day.
Today Paddy is the King

Answering only to the name King Patrick, Paddy empties the linen cupboard, rearranges all the furniture, builds an enormous castle using the sheets off all the freshly made beds and insists Mum sits in the castle.

Friday

Today is no ordinary day.
Today is an extraordinary day.
Today Paddy is a firefighter.

Driving a fire truck, Paddy searches the house for fires, he uses mum's phone to call for back up, swings the fire hose around and climbs the chair and table to reach the fires high up.

Saturday

Today is no ordinary day.
Today is an extraordinary day.
Today Paddy is a plumber.

Ready with his toolbox Paddy the plumber gets to work in the bathroom tightening taps, repairing the drain and mopping up spills with the freshly washed towels.

Sunday

Today is no ordinary day.
Today is an extraordinary day.
Today Paddy is a gardener

Prepared with his gardening clothes, Paddy gets to work in the backyard. He waters the newly sprouted carrots, does the weeding, mows the lawn and pulls all the small green fruit off the orange tree.